Editor
Barbara M. Wally, M.S.

Editorial Manager
Ina Massler Levin, M.A.

Editor-in-Chief
Sharon Coan, M.S. Ed.

Cover Artist
Sue Fullam

Art Coordinator
Cheri Macoubrie Wilson

Creative Director
Elayne Roberts

Imaging
Ralph Olmedo, Jr.

Product Manager
Phil Garcia

Publisher
Mary D. Smith, M.S. Ed.

How to Write a Paragraph

Grades 1–3

Author

Kathleen Christopher Null

Teacher Created Resources, Inc.
6421 Industry Way
Westminster, CA 92683
www.teachercreated.com

ISBN: 978-1-57690-494-7

©1999 Teacher Created Resources, Inc.
Reprinted, 2013

Made in U.S.A.

Table of Contents

Introduction

Knowing how to write a clear and well-organized paragraph is the foundation for success in any future writing that students experience. When students realize that longer pieces of writing are written one paragraph at a time, they will become capable and confident writers.

This book will enable you to take the essential unit of good writing, the paragraph, and teach it to your students in its many forms. The activities may be modified to your students' abilities and needs, using the variations at the bottom of each page or your own adaptations. (Cover the "For Younger Students" text before duplicating each page.)

Getting Started

Getting Started section, you will find pages to introduce the basic concepts of paragraph writing. Included are pre-writing activities, such as generating ideas and brainstorming.

Paragraph Parts

Next you will find a section on the Paragraph Parts, which includes the basics of main ideas, topic sentences, supporting and body sentences, transitions, and conclusions.

Kinds of Paragraphs

This section introduces seven different kinds of paragraph writing: narration, explanation, description, comparison and contrast, persuasion, opinion, and definition. An activity is provided for each one.

Paragraph Practice

This section will give students the opportunity to practice all that they have learned so far. The paragraph starters in this section can be used in many different ways and whenever you wish. In addition, they will make good story starters.

Putting Paragraphs Together

In this section, students will be introduced to the basics of letter and essay writing, as they learn to put paragraphs together to create longer forms of writing.

Paragraph Plans

In this section you will find a worksheet which can be used frequently until students are confident about writing paragraphs. A post-writing checklist is also included for students to check their own paragraphs to make sure they have included the essentials.

Fun with Paragraphs

Your students will be rewarded for their diligence with the fun activities in this section, which will also act as a review of the concepts they have learned.

When your students have completed this book, they will be on their way to being creative and capable writers who understand the importance of the paragraph to their writing projects.

What Is a Paragraph?

A paragraph is a short piece of writing that has a beginning, a middle, and an end. Have you ever seen a patchwork quilt? Did you notice that it is made of lots of little pieces that have been stitched together? You wouldn't have a big, warm patchwork quilt without all the little squares. Every story, essay, article, or book is made of little paragraphs "stitched" together. When you know how to write a paragraph, you know how to do lots of different kinds of writing.

Now that you have an idea about how a paragraph works, here are the basics.

The Beginning

When you talk to your friends, you begin by getting their interest. You might say, "Hey, guess what!" or "You won't believe this!" Then you let them know what it is that you are going to talk about: "I saw something yesterday that you will want to know about." *The very first sentence of your paragraph is called a topic sentence.* A topic sentence tells what your paragraph will be about. "I have a dog" is a topic sentence, but it's not as interesting as "I have a talking dog." The second sentence gives readers more information about what your paragraph will be about and will make them want to read your paragraph.

The Middle

After you have your friends' attention, you tell them the details. *In your paragraph, the sentences that follow your topic sentence, also known as body sentences, add interesting details and explain what you mean.* Each sentence needs to be about your topic. If the topic is your talking dog, you won't have a sentence telling about your math test. Instead, you might write, "My dog knows how to say, 'Mama' and 'wanna'." You might also tell how the dog learned the words.

The End

The last sentence of your paragraph is the concluding sentence, or closing sentence. This sentence will remind your reader of what you are writing about and what it means to you. You might end your paragraph about your talking dog by saying, "It may not seem like he is talking like humans do, but if you listen closely and have some cheese, you will hear the words, and you will be amazed!"

Remember, every paragraph, just like every story or book, has a beginning, a middle, and an end.

4

▲▼ ▲▼ ▲▼ ▲▼ ▲▼ ▲▼ ▲▼ ▲▼ ▶

Lots of Ideas

To write a paragraph, you need an idea. A good way to get ideas is to ask lots of questions. What do you wonder about? Why is the grass green? What if it were purple instead? What makes you laugh? What would it be like to live underground? Keep a notebook for writing down all of your questions and ideas. Here's a page to get you started. Answer the questions below. (You may not have the answers to some of them, but write what comes to your mind and you may learn more about what interests you). Later, you may want to use these ideas for writing paragraphs, stories, or reports.

What is your favorite animal? _____

Why does it snow? _____

Why do we have bugs? _____

What is your favorite holiday? Why? _____

If you were to invent a candy, what would it be like?

_____

Would you like to go to space? _____

Challenge: Keep a "What If?" notebook. Record all the "what if" questions you can think of, such as, "What if there were no gravity?" or "What if we could trade places with our parents?" When you have time to write or you need inspiration for a journal entry, use an idea from your "what if" notebook.

For Younger Students: Have students list three things about which they are curious (example: bugs, roller coasters, dinosaurs, etc.) Have them think of one question that they would like to ask about each subject. (For instance, "What is the tallest roller coaster in the world?") They can write each question (with help as required) at the bottom of a sheet of paper and fill in the remaining space with an illustration. Post these around the room to keep the curiosity going; and when they are ready, help the children find the answers to their questions.

A Storm in Your Brain!

Thinking of new ideas is like having a storm in your brain! You need to write the ideas before they flash and disappear. You can brainstorm by yourself, with the class, your friends, or your parents. Here are the rules for brainstorming:

1. Write down all the ideas.
2. Don't think about whether you like them or not, just write them down.
3. Let all the ideas come out—they don't need to make sense.
4. When you are finished and no more ideas are coming, look at your ideas and circle the ones you like best.

Here is a list of words that some students wrote when they were thinking about the word "play":

> fun, after school, all summer long, play clothes, toys, basketball, dolls, silly, laughing, jumping, exciting, friends, backyard, park, swimming pools, slides, jungle gym, recess, games, jump rope, hopscotch

The students used the words to write paragraphs. Here is what one student wrote about her favorite things to do after school with her friends.

I love to play after school with Mindy and Heather. We play dress-up and even put clothes on Mindy's cat. Sometimes we jump rope on Heather's big, smooth driveway. Sometimes we go to my house and play dolls with my little sisters. We play until our mothers call us to come in. Then we have to work.

On the back of this paper, brainstorm a list of ideas for the word "vacation." Your teacher may have you do this with a partner or with the whole class.

Challenge: If you think you are ready, use your brainstormed list or the one above to write a paragraph.

For Younger Students: Play word association games as a whole class or in partners. You may wish to prepare some word lists in advance. Explain to students that coming up with related words quickly is a form of brainstorming.

All the Right Stuff

A paragraph is like a mini-story. Just like a story, it has a beginning, a middle and an end.

The Beginning

The first sentence of a paragraph is called a topic sentence because it tells what the paragraph will be about. Here is an example of a topic sentence:

My dog thinks she is a human.

The Middle

All of the sentences that come after the topic sentence tell more about the topic. For example:

First of all, she can open doors. She jumps up and opens the door with her paws, and then she walks into the house to see if there is anything to eat. After that, she makes herself comfortable on the couch.

The End

The last sentence of your paragraph is the closing or conclusion. This sentence can say what the paragraph is about and tell what it means to you. Here is a closing sentence for the paragraph above:

And so, my dog thinks she is human, and I haven't told her that she is a dog because I don't want to hurt her feelings.

Can you fill in the middle sentences in this paragraph?

I love birthday parties!

I get really excited when I get a birthday party invitation!

Challenge: Write the closing sentence for a paragraph. Trade with a partner and have him of her write the beginning and middle parts while you do the same. Did he or she write what you had in mind?

For Younger Students: Using the paragraph, write the first sentence and the beginning of the second sentence, and allow the student to orally fill in the rest of the paragraph as you write his or her words at your prompt. When completed, allow students to draw a picture to illustrate their birthday paragraphs.

What's the Big Idea?

A paragraph should tell the reader about one idea. If you have lots of ideas, you will need to write lots of paragraphs. Each paragraph needs just one main idea.

In the Ideas Bank below, you will find four ideas or topics. There are four lists on this page that need a main idea. Take the ideas from the box and write them at the top of the lists below.

Ideas Bank

favorite foods	toys
summer	television

---

1. The Main Idea: _____

    cartoons on Saturday morning   movies   my favorite show

2. The Main Idea: _____

    pizza   French fries   nuggets

3. The Main Idea: _____

    trains   squirt guns   basketballs

4. The Main Idea: _____

    swimming   vacations   no school

Challenge: Cut out the main ideas and the items from each list (enlarging them first might be a good idea). You should have 20 slips of paper. Mix them up and see if you can arrange them with the main ideas and the details together. A matching game could also be played with these ideas. If two slips of paper are related, they may be taken. If not, turn them back over and let the next player try.

For Younger Students: Use the four main ideas and, as a class, have students brainstorm words and ideas that are related. For instance, "favorite foods" would inspire many responses about their personal favorites. Be sure they understand that they are brainstorming for ideas and details about a topic.

Find the Big Idea

The boxes on the left side of the page are full of ideas. Each box on the right side of the page contains a main idea. Draw a line connecting the box of ideas with its matching main idea.

Ideas   **Main Ideas**

shirts	socks
shoes	pajamas

rain	fog
snow	wind

spaghetti	ice cream
cookies	apples

table	rug
sink	spoon

things we find at home

weather

things we eat

things we wear

Challenge: Can you list four ideas after each of the big ideas in this list?

My favorite sports:_____

_____

Why candy is important: _____

_____

For Younger Students: Find clip art to represent things we find at home (e.g., articles of clothing, food, etc.). On a flannelboard, create columns or sections with headings, such as "Things We Wear," "Things We Eat," etc. Allow students to group the items in the appropriate sections. Explain to them that paragraphs are groupings of related ideas, too.

▲▽▲▽▲▽▲▽▲▽▲▽▲▽▲▽▲▽

Sticking to the Point

This page is all about camping. On this page you will find sentences about camping that might go into a paragraph about camping. You will also find sentences that are not about camping. Cross out the sentences that are not about the topic of camping.

Camping is fun.

It's fun to sleep outside or in a tent.

The most popular sport on my street is soccer.

Food tastes better when it has been cooked over a fire.

We make s'mores with graham crackers, marshmallows, and chocolate!

I can play outside after I clean up my room.

Sometimes we might see a deer from our campsite.

We can hike and fish.

If I finish my homework, I can watch my favorite TV show.

It doesn't matter if I get dirty while I am camping.

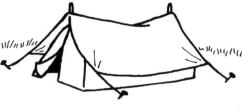

My dog knows how to shake and sit.

I like to sleep in a cozy sleeping bag.

Challenge: When you finish crossing out what doesn't belong, circle your favorite ideas about camping and, on the back of this page or on another piece of paper, write a paragraph that includes those ideas.

For Younger Students: This activity would be fun as a whole class oral exercise. Using either the "Camping Is Fun" theme or one of your choosing, list related and/or unrelated sub-topics. Have students stand, sit, or give thumbs up or thumbs down (or the signal of your choice) to say whether the ideas are related or not. Emphasize the concept of sticking to the point.

What I Want to Say Is . . .

Do you remember what a topic sentence is? It's the first sentence of a paragraph and it says what the paragraph will be about. Read this paragraph and then circle the topic sentence.

I love a big, fat chair. I can curl up in a big, fat chair and read a book. I can take a nap in a big, fat chair. I can't think of a better place to be than in a big, fat chair!

The topic of the paragraph is "big, fat chair." What the writer wants to say about big, fat chairs is that he or she loves a big, fat chair.

What would you like to say about the topics below? Write a topic sentence to show what you would like to say. The first two have been completed to give you ideas.

1. Vegetables <u>Vegetables are yucky.</u> _____

2. Cats <u>I like to hear cats purr.</u> _____

3. Books _____

4. Music _____

5. Cars _____

Challenge: Choose your favorite topic sentence from this page and try writing a paragraph about the topic.

For Younger Students: Prepare handouts with unfinished sentences across the bottom of the page. For example, you might use prompts like "Vegetables are," "Dogs are," "School is," etc. Have students finish the sentences by making a point (they may dictate to you if they need to). Have them illustrate their topics. Emphasize that this is their opportunity to make a point, voice an opinion, and write a topic sentence!

▼▲▼▲▼▲▼▲▼▲▼▲▼▲▼

What I Want to Say Is . . . *(cont.)*

Now that you've had some practice with thinking up topic sentences, see if you can find a topic sentence for each of these paragraphs. You may choose a topic sentence from the bank or make up one of your own. Write it on the line above the paragraph

---

Topics Bank

Cats are lazy animals.	I love dessert!	I like to run.
I don't like to wear shoes.	A dinosaur lives under my bed.	It's not good to eat too much.

_____

There are so many choices. There's ice cream, cake, pie, and cookies. I think brownies are my favorite. I wish I could just eat only desserts and never spinach!

_____

I can hear him snoring at night. In the daytime he goes outside and eats my mom's daisies. He tracked his muddy footprints into the house. I ask for extra macaroni and cheese to feed my dinosaur.

_____

They pinch my feet. I can't wiggle my toes as much as I want to. My feet get hot in shoes. I can't wait until summer when my feet can come out to play.

Challenge: Write a topic sentence. Make it goofy, silly, or very mysterious. Exchange sentences with a partner and write a paragraph to go with the topic sentence your partner wrote, while he or she writes one to go with yours.

For Younger Students: Put each topic sentence on a sentence strip and each paragraph on a piece of poster or butcher paper. As a class, read each topic sentence aloud; then read each paragraph to see if it matches the topic sentence just read. Have students guess which paragraph goes with which topic sentence and place the pairs, when matched, on a chart so students can look at them more closely throughout the week.

Let Me Explain

A topic sentence is very important, but it can't do its job without help. The sentences that come after a topic sentence help by explaining the topic. If your best friend ran up to you and shouted, "The nose is missing!" and then ran away again, you'd wonder what he was talking about. The topic sentence he shouted was interesting and important, but it needs an explanation. Later he explains that the nose to his rocket is missing.

Here are some topic sentences that need to be explained. Choose the explanation from the body sentences bank to explain what the topic sentence means. Put an A, B, or C in the box after each topic sentence below.

Topic Sentences:

1. I crushed a car!_____

2. I thought the bathtub would be a good place to keep my frog.

    _____

3. My sister wanted to eat a bug._____

A. Then I head my mom scream. She came out in her bathrobe and yelled, "Who put a frog in the bathtub?" I tried to explain that it just had to stay there until Monday when I would take it to school. But she made me put it in a big jar with holes punched in the top. Then she made me scrub the bathtub. I guess it wasn't such a good idea.

B. She crawled on a blanket in the back yard and picked up the plastic blocks and chewed on them. When she saw a bug crawl onto the blanket, she dropped the plastic blocks and started to reach for the bug. I was just watching, but my mom ran out and grabbed the bug and tossed it into the bushes.

C. I didn't mean to. I was running into the house and my little brother's tiny, plastic car was in the way. I accidentally stepped on it and crushed it. He cried. I have to buy him a new one with my allowance.

▼▲▼▲▼▲▼▲▼▲▼▲▼▲▼▲

Let Me Explain *(cont.)*

Here are two paragraphs that are missing explanations. Can you add them? If you need help, you can look at the idea bank at the bottom of the page.

Ferris wheels are a lot of fun. They are fun because _____

They are also fun because _____

_____ I really like Ferris wheels.

One of my friends is really a robot. I think he is a robot because_____

_____

It's also strange that _____

_____ I'm sure he's a robot!

Idea Bank

they go really high	he talks funny
they are colorful	I've never seen him eat food
they go around and around	I've never seen him cry
they have pretty lights on them	I don't think he has a tongue

---

Challenge: See if you can write a really strange topic sentence that can be explained later. (Be sure to have a good explanation!) Gather strange topic sentences from all your classmates, and have your teacher read them aloud. Try to guess what the author meant. When you have had enough guessing, the author needs to explain what he or she means.

For Younger Students: As a class, give each student an opportunity to explain something. For instance, ask one student why she likes to wear red sneakers, and allow her to give as many reasons as she can. Let the students know that being able to explain something is an important part of writing.

I Need Some Body to Help

Every paragraph needs a body. The sentences that come after the topic sentence (the beginning) and before the closing sentence (the end) are the *body sentences*, and they are in the body of the paragraph (the middle). The body sentences are about the topic; they explain the topic with details like who, what, where, why, and how.

Here is a paragraph that is missing its body sentences. Can you fill them in? You can make up the sentences yourself, or use the body sentence bank below for ideas. (Be careful: Some of the sentences in the sentence bank are for another paragraph!)

I like to go to the park. _____

_____

_____

_____

_____

_____ The park is my favorite place to be.

Body Sentence Bank

There are 11 different swings at the park.

There are some twisty slides at the park.

I can have a picnic on the grass.

I like to play in the sandbox next to the swings.

Spelling is my favorite subject in school.

My teacher is really nice.

I like to play kickball during recess.

There are some really good trees for climbing at the park.

I Need Some Body to Help *(cont.)*

Here is a paragraph that is missing some parts. The three reasons that explain the topic (the body sentences) are missing. Can you fill them in? Be sure to use complete sentences.

I would like to live in Disneyland for three reasons. The first reason is

_____

Another reason is _____

Finally, if I lived in Disneyland _____

_____ I would love to live in Disneyland!

Extension: Try more paragraphs on a separate piece of paper. Here are some topic sentences to try.

I would like a tree house in my backyard for three reasons.

I like cats for the following four reasons.

There are three reasons I would not eat a snail—even for one hundred dollars.

Challenge: Using the sentences about school from the sentence bank on the previous page, write a paragraph by creating a topic sentence, a closing sentence, and any body sentences that you think should be added to complete the paragraph.

For Younger Students: Write the sentences from the previous page on large sentence strips. Give each strip to a student. Have the students come forward with their strips, and ask them to arrange themselves to make a paragraph. (You may need to read the sentences aloud before they begin to move about.) When they think that they are finished with their strips, read the paragraph aloud and edit the paragraph as a class. Does the order make sense? Should it be rearranged? Are there any sentences that don't seem to belong?

Next?

When you are talking or writing about something that happened to you, you usually tell it in the order that it happened: Putting things in order by time is called chronological (kron-ah-lodge-ah-kal) order. Directions and recipes are also written in the chronological order of how they should be done.

Here are some things that are out of order. Put them in order by writing the numbers 1, 2, or 3, in the spaces below. The first one has been done for you.

Mornings

<u>3</u> go to school

<u>1</u> wake up

<u>2</u> eat breakfast

Eating Cereal

_____ get a bowl

_____ pour the milk

_____ pour the cereal

Going to Camp

_____ get on the bus

_____ kiss parents good-bye

_____ pack a bag

Baking a Cake

_____ put it in the oven

_____ pour the batter in the pan

_____ mix the batter

Challenge: Illustrate the event stories on cards. Use one card for each detail. Mix them up and let another student put them in order. Take your chronological story cards to the kindergarten classroom and explain to them what chronological order means. Have them arrange the story cards in order. Make more event stories and cards with your own ideas

For Younger Students: Create cards for event stories. Have the students illustrate the events and place them in chronological order.

And Then . . .

Listen very carefully the next time you hear someone talking about something that happened to them. You might hear something like this:

"I got in line for the elephant ride <u>and then</u> I waited, <u>and pretty soon</u> it was my turn. I tried to get up on the elephant, <u>but</u> I couldn't reach. The man got a little ladder, <u>and then</u> I could reach. <u>Next</u>, I was on top of the elephant, <u>and suddenly</u> it started to walk. I was frightened, <u>so</u> I started yelling, 'Stop,' <u>but then</u> the elephant just went faster. I started to cry <u>and</u> the man came over. The man said that I scared the elephant when I yelled, <u>and then</u> he brought the elephant and me back to the start. <u>Finally</u>, I climbed off the elephant, <u>and</u> as soon as I got back to my mom, I told her that I scared the elephant <u>and</u> she started to laugh."

All the underlined words connect the things that happened in this story. They are words like "and so," "first," "suddenly," "today," "and then," "and "finally." These are connecting words, or transitions.

In the story below, circle all the connecting words or transitions that you can find.

Today I woke up early, and then I brushed my teeth. Next, I put my homework in my backpack, and then I put my books in, too. I ate breakfast but then I noticed that it was really quiet. First, I went to my mom's room, but she was still sleeping. Next, I went to my brother's room, but he was really asleep. After that, I went to the porch, and even the dog was still sleeping. Suddenly, I remembered it was Saturday, so I went back to bed!

Challenge: Write a story and leave out all the transition words. Read it aloud to see how it sounds without them. Trade stories with a partner and add the transitions for each other.

For Younger Students: Read the story aloud, putting emphasis on all transitional words or phrases.

Give the students something to do, on subsequent readings, when they hear a transitional word or phrase, for instance, standing, raising their hands, speaking the words or phrases aloud as you come to them.

▲▼ ▲▼ ▲▼ ▲▼ ▲▼ ▲▼ ▲▼ ▲▼ ▶

And So . . .

Every story has an ending, and so do paragraphs. The last sentence, or the last few sentences of a paragraph, is called the *closing sentence*, or the conclusion. All you need to remember is to finish your paragraphs with a feeling, a thought, an attitude, or a point you want to make.

Here is a paragraph that has no ending:

I like to go to the store with my mom. I get to pick out the apples.
I also get to choose a cereal just for me. I like to smell the
peaches.

Here are some endings that might work for this unfinished paragraph. Circle the one that you like the best.

I get so hungry at the store that I can't wait to bring the food home!

My mom lets me pick out some peaches, and then we go home and make a fruit salad.

After we finish, my mom lets me get some gum before we go home.

I help put the food in the bags, and then we take it all home.

Challenge: Write some paragraph starts of 3–4 sentences and exchange them. Write an ending to a paragraph that you didn't start. Write one paragraph start for all students in the class. See how many different endings are created.

For Younger Students: Read the paragraph aloud and let each student choose the ending he or she likes best. Then read the completed paragraphs. You may wish to create a handout of the paragraph, and when the last sentence is added, students can create an illustration that shows the closing sentence they chose.

Story Time!

When you go home and someone asks you what happened at school today, you will probably tell your story starting with the first thing that happened and finishing with what happened on the way home. Telling or writing about an experience or event in a detailed story form is called *narrative*. It tells what happened in chronological order. When you write about something that you did or something that happened, you are writing in narrative form.

In the paragraph below, choose one of the main ideas in the parentheses and circle it. Write sentences that add details about the topic in narrative form.

The first time I (rode a bike, went swimming, roller skated, flew on a plane) was a total disaster.

First, _____

Next, _____

Then, _____

Finally, _____

Copy the following sentence on a piece of lined paper, choosing one of the events in the parentheses. Add details to write a narrative paragraph about your topic.

> On my (first day of school, last birthday, last vacation), I . . .

Challenge: Observe the many ways that narrative is used all around you every day. Find it in stories, on the radio, in magazines, on the television, in movies, and in the things that your friends and family say as they tell stories. Collect or write down some examples to bring to class for a narrative display.

For Younger Students: Ask each student to dictate what he or she did over the weekend or the night before. Write what he or she says. Explain that they have just told you a story in narrative form. Have them illustrate their stories.

Please Explain

When you write a paragraph that gives facts, explains ideas, or gives directions, you are writing an *expository* paragraph. Expository (*x-PAUSE-eh-tory*) means writing that exposes or explains something.

A lot of the writing in a newspaper is expository—so are research reports, recipes, directions, and a letter to your parents explaining why you should be able to stay up later.

When you give an oral report that is full of facts, explanations, or directions, that is an expository report. Choose one of these topics and be prepared to verbally explain it to the class.

Tell how to take a bath.

Give the facts about your favorite book or
    cartoon character.

Explain how to skate.

Tell the facts about your pet.

Share how to bake a birthday cake.

Tell why you like ice cream.

Explain how to wash your hair.

Explain how to make a peanut butter sandwich.

Tell how to play your favorite game.

Explain the rules of your favorite sport.

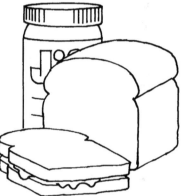

Challenge: Pick another topic and write an expository paragraph. For more of a challenge, choose a topic and write four expository paragraphs about the topic.

For Younger Students: Tape record responses to topics such as "Tell why you like pizza." The tapes can be placed in a learning center for students to listen to. Some may want to illustrate their explanations.

Describe It!

When you run into the house and say that there is a really huge, green dinosaur in the front yard, you are describing the dinosaur so everyone will know what it looks like. The words, "really huge" and "green" paint a picture in our minds. A descriptive paragraph paints a picture of what things look, smell, taste, feel and sound like. Some of these paragraphs are descriptive and some are not. Draw a circle around the descriptive paragraphs.

My dog is in the backyard. I am in the house. My sister is doing her homework. I want to go outside and play with my dog, but first I have to finish eating my peas.

There is a fuzzy, orange spider creeping and crawling along the dirty window sill. I want to scream, but my great big brother, who is tired after a horrible day of football practice, might wake up if I make a very loud and sudden noise! Instead of screaming, I am slowly moving away, and I can taste the salty sweat rolling down onto my lips.

It will soon be my birthday. I want a skateboard and a helmet. I will have a cake and some ice cream. My friends will come over and spend the night.

My seventh birthday is next week! I want a pair of purple and silver roller blades and green elbow pads. I'm going to have banana and chocolate cake with fudge frosting and fudge ripple ice cream. My best friends will come over and stay all night long.

Challenge: Take out a piece of paper and write a paragraph that describes everything you can sense with your five senses about where you are right now.

For Younger Students: Have some students dress up in hats, gloves, jackets, etc. Either one at a time or all at once, have the dressed-up students enter the classroom, walk across the room, and then exit. When they are gone, have students verbally describe the students. For a variation, have them draw what they saw.

Different and the Same

When you say to your mom, "I'm taller than you, but we have the same hair color," you are comparing and contrasting. Think of contrast as black and white, or opposites. You are tall; your mother is short. Comparing is finding what is the same or similar. "My hamster's fur is the same color as your hair!"

When you write a paragraph that compares what is the same about two things or contrasts what is different, it is a comparison or contrast paragraph. Sometimes you will both compare and contrast: You are tall, and your mom is short, but you both have the same hair color. A good way to prepare to write a comparison/contrast paragraph is to fill in a Venn diagram. Think of a friend or family member who is like you in some ways and different from you in other ways. Fill in the diagram below with the things that are the same and the things that are different.

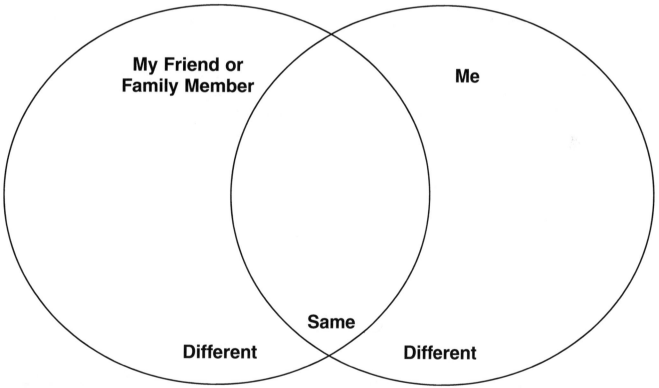

Challenge: Write a paragraph or a multi-paragraph essay comparing and contrasting yourself with the friend or family member you chose for the Venn diagram.

For Younger Students: As a class, compare various objects (e.g., different kinds of fruit, bread, plants, or leaves) and chart the differences on poster-size Venn diagrams. Demonstrate writing a paragraph that compares and contrasts the items selected.

I'm Right!

Have you ever felt strongly about something and wanted to convince others that you were right? A persuasive paragraph uses examples, details, and evidence to prove that you are right. Let's say that you want to convince your parents to get you a puppy. You might write or say some of the following things:

I will take good care of him.

I will build a doghouse and take him for a walk every morning before school and every day after school.

He'll be a good watchdog. Juan's dog was trained to be a watchdog.

I'll train him to bring in the paper.

He'll go wherever I go and protect me.

Doctors say that children with dogs are healthier and happier.

Cut out the topic strips below and mix them up. With a partner or a team, take turns drawing a topic from a box. When it is your turn, look at your topic and think of four reasons why you are right about your topic. For instance, if your topic is "Elephants are cute," you might say, "They have fuzzy heads; they have big, cute feet; when they give themselves a shower, they look funny; and when they eat it looks like they are smiling." After you try to persuade your partner or team, ask if they are convinced or not. If not, draw another topic. If they are convinced, it's your partner's or team member's turn. Take turns until you've tried all the topics.

The ocean is fun.	Vegetables are yucky.
We should never have homework.	The ocean is scary.
Carrots are really good.	We should have homework every night.
We need to wear shoes.	We don't need to wear shoes.

Challenge: Choose a topic and write a letter to someone to convince him or her that you're right. Pretend that the person you are writing to disagrees with you.

For Younger Students: As a class, brainstorm for convincing arguments to prove the point of your choice. Choose one from above or come up with one of your own. Allow each student to contribute at least one convincing detail on the topic.

That's What I Like!

Everyone has opinions, even you! An opinion paragraph is your chance to say what you think about a topic. What do you think of ice cream? Do you like it? Do you like it a lot? Do you hate it? Why? Here is an example:

There are three reasons why I dislike my doctor. First, I dislike my doctor because I have to wait for a long time to see him, and there is nothing to do. Second, I dislike my doctor because he puts a really cold thing in my ear and on my chest. And finally, I dislike my doctor because he gives me shots, and they hurt. I really do dislike my doctor because he is so mean to me.

Think of a topic about which you have an opinion and brainstorm, writing down every idea you can think of about your topic. When you are finished brainstorming, circle your three best ideas.

Circle whether you like or dislike the topic and fill in the spaces in this paragraph to write an opinion paragraph.

There are three reasons why I (like/dislike) _____

First, I (like/dislike) _____ because _____

Second, I (like/dislike) _____ because _____

And finally, I (like/dislike) _____ because _____

I really do (like/dislike) _____.

Challenge: After you have written an opinion paragraph, try writing it again, with the opposite opinion. For example, the person who wrote about disliking his or her doctor would write an opinion paragraph about why he or she likes the doctor.

For Younger Students: Create a chart with slots for word strips. Design the chart so that it shows the format for an opinion paragraph (see above). Create sentence strips, and topics, to fit in the blanks. Allow students to rearrange the sentence strips and to choose different topics about which they have opinions.

What Is This?

Can you tell us all about your favorite food without saying what that food is? You might say what it looks like, what it tastes like, how it smells, how it feels, etc. You would be defining your favorite food. If you were to write about what your favorite food is like, you'd be writing a *definition*. A paragraph that defines something is called a definitive paragraph.

Match each of the definitive paragraphs with a topic from the box below. Write the topic on the line after the paragraph.

It looks like worms! It's slimy and slithery and rolling around in tomatoes or meatballs. It tastes wonderful but it's messy. _____

It's really big and green, but on the inside it's red and polka-dotted with lots of little black seeds. The outside is hard, and the inside is wet and squishy. It tastes wonderful in the summertime, but it's really drippy. _____

It's small and brown but can come in other colors. It has little ears, button eyes, and whiskers. It has a bow around its neck. It's fuzzy and cuddly and likes to be hugged. It makes me feel better if I'm sick or scared. It sleeps with me in my bed. _____

It's about the size of my foot, and it might be made of leather or rubber. It has straps, and I like to wear it in the summer. It's not at all like a boot. Some of these make flip-flopping sounds when I walk. _____

Topics: a sandal	a watermelon	a teddy bear	spaghetti

Challenge: Choose three topics from this list: *a scary place, the ocean, the forest, soup, a bicycle, a funny place, a grandparent, a pet*. Write a description for each one, using as many of the five senses as you can. Read your descriptions aloud in class, but do not reveal your topic until the end.

For Younger Students: Have students bring in favorite objects for show and tell. Have them keep their objects hidden while they describe them to the class. When they are finished describing, their classmates can guess what the object is.

Mud!

Your paragraph assignment fell in the mud on the way to school. You can read some of what you wrote. The rest is covered in mud! Now you'll have to write parts of your paragraph over again.

I like everything about ice cream, but there are three things I especially like. One of my favorite things is

_____

because _____

_____

Another thing I really like is_____

_____

because _____

_____

Finally, I like _____

_____

because _____

_____

I'm so glad there is ice cream!

Sticky Glue!

Oh no! Now you left your paragraph on the table. You didn't know that your sister left sticky glue all over the table. When you picked up the paper—yuck— lots of your paragraph stayed glued to the table. Now you will have to fill in the missing parts of your paragraph.

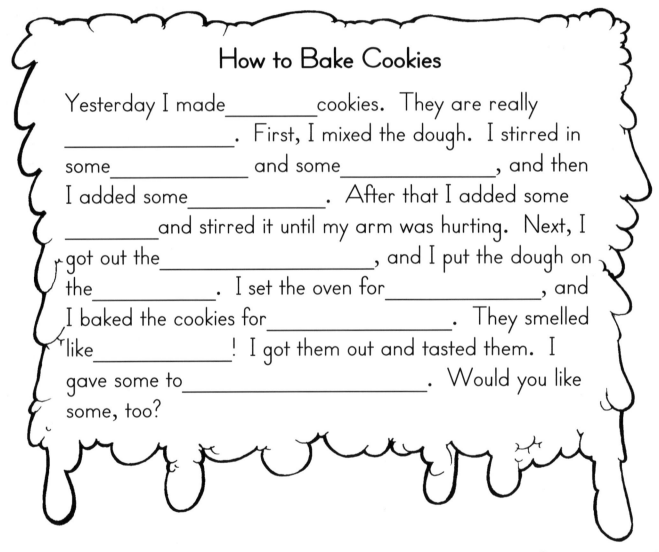

How to Bake Cookies

Yesterday I made_____cookies. They are really _____. First, I mixed the dough. I stirred in some_____ and some_____, and then I added some_____. After that I added some _____and stirred it until my arm was hurting. Next, I got out the_____, and I put the dough on the_____. I set the oven for_____, and I baked the cookies for_____. They smelled like_____! I got them out and tasted them. I gave some to_____. Would you like some, too?

Challenge: Find some paragraphs in magazines or newspapers. Cross out some of the words and ask a partner to give you new words to use instead. Read your new paragraph aloud. Write a paragraph that is missing some parts. Exchange paragraphs with your classmates. Finish the new paragraph that was passed to you. Read the paragraphs aloud. Were the paragraphs different from what the original author intended?

For Younger Students: Provide pages with partially-written paragraphs and take dictation while helping students fill them in with their own, original ideas.

My Favorite Thing to Do

What is your favorite thing to do after school? Choose an idea from the idea bank or come up with your own idea. When you have an idea, finish the paragraph.

Idea Bank		
roller skate	play a sport	ride my bike
swim	play with dolls	read
jump rope	draw	talk to my friends
play games	write letters	skateboard
climb trees	play with clay	play on the playground

My Favorite Thing to Do

My favorite thing to do after school is _____

I like to _____ because _____

_____

Another reason that I like to _____ is because

_____

_____

Finally, I like to _____ because _____

_____

Challenge: Choose three things that you like to do after school, in the summertime, or in the winter. Write three paragraphs, one for each activity.

For Younger Students: Make this a whole-class activity. Begin with students brainstorming what they like to do. Write their ideas on the board or on chart paper. Prepare a paragraph form (similar to the one on this page) and make it poster size. With input from the students, model how to use the information from the brainstormed list to write a paragraph.

Paragraph Starters

Use these paragraph starters when you need an idea while practicing paragraph writing. You can also use these ideas for writing longer pieces or stories.

I like bugs.	I don't like green things.
There are so many things shaped like a circle.	My favorite color is . . .
I would like to be invisible.	I am glad to be in my family because . . .
My favorite food is . . .	I should have my own room.
I would like to join the circus.	I would like to travel in space.
I would like to be able to stop time.	I don't like cats.
I would like a giraffe for a pet.	I am glad that I have thumbs because . . .
It would be nice to have a Ferris wheel in my backyard.	Gravity should be turned off at night.
I would like a puppy.	I will never eat a _____ because . . .

Paragraph Starters *(cont.)*

I like snakes because . . .	I would like to be a fish.
It would be more fun to live in a tent.	I love merry-go-rounds.
Yellow is the best color for food.	If I had a fairy godmother . . .
I don't like to draw because . . .	I would not like to lose my nose.
I'd rather be barefooted.	Rain is important.
I wish I could drive a car because . . .	I love books.
A hairy monster lives in my closet.	I would like to travel to . . .
I like ketchup.	I don't like snails because . . .
I don't like wind.	I like tree houses.
It's always a good idea to wear a hat.	Bicycles are great because . . .
I am afraid of big dogs.	Pets are a good idea because . . .

Essays Are Easy!

If you can write a paragraph, you can write an essay! An essay is a piece of writing that is made up of several paragraphs. Like a paragraph, an essay has a beginning (an introductory paragraph), a middle (body paragraphs) and an ending (concluding paragraph).

Here is an example of a short essay on the topic of crayons:

I Love Crayons!

I got my first box of crayons when I was four years old, and I have loved them ever since! I love the colors, the way they smell, and what I can do with them. My mom sometimes buys me a new box of crayons to add to my collection.

When I open a new box of crayons, I am amazed at the colors. There are silver, indigo, and lime crayons. There are even crayons that are not only the color of watermelons or blueberries, but smell like them, too! Even when they don't smell like fruit, I like how they smell. That waxy smell means I get to draw some new pictures.

I also like to make scratch art and melt the leftover pieces to make "stained glass windows." Sometimes I use my crayons to write a pretty note to my mom.

So, I really love crayons, and I always will. The colors are amazing and I can do lots of things with them. Now that I have written an essay about crayons, maybe my mom will buy me some more!

Challenge: Find examples of essays at the library. Can you see how the topic is introduced? Does the author use specific details in the body paragraphs? Can you find the conclusion?

For Younger Students: Enlarge the example paragraph on poster board. Give each student a copy of the example paragraph and four crayons. Read the essay aloud to the students. Next, describe the parts of the essay and color each part a different color.

Essays Are Easy! *(cont.)*

Now it's your turn to write a short essay! Choose a topic from the Paragraph Starters (pages 30–31) or create one of your own. Your essay will have four paragraphs. Fill in the boxes below to create your own essay. If you need help, see the sample short essay on page 32, titled, "I Love Crayons!"

Title	
Topic and Introduction	
First Body Paragraph (Add lots of details about your topic, here.)	
Second Body Paragraph (Add more details here.)	
Concluding Paragraph (What does it mean to you? What is your point?)	

Challenge: Using another piece of paper, write a five- or six-paragraph essay about something that makes you mad, glad, or sad.

For Younger Students: Using the paragraph form on this page, you may wish to have some students draw in each box to demonstrate what they want to say about their topics. Guide them in making their illustrations. Show such things as an introduction to their topic (for instance, in the crayon essay, the introductory box might show the four-year-old receiving her first crayons), the details, etc. Or, you may wish to have students share their essays orally.

What Is a Letter?

Do you like to get letters from friends or family? Do you sometimes send letters? A letter is a kind of essay! In a letter, the beginning is called the *salutation*, or greeting. The middle is the body, and the end is the closing and the signature. Each paragraph of a letter is about a different topic.

Here is an example of a letter. At the end of each paragraph, there is a box. Choose the paragraph's topic from the topic box below and put its number in the box.

Beginning
(Salutation or greeting)

Middle
(Body)

End
(Closing and signature)

> July 8, 2003
>
> Dear Mom and Dad,
> They told us we have to write a letter home tonight. They tell us to do a lot of things around here. Yesterday they told us we all had to jump in the lake. It was really cold. ☐
> Can you also bring me some real food? All we have to eat here are things like oatmeal, salads, and fruit. The only things to drink are water, fruit juices, and milk. ☐
> We've been hiking, and climbing and boating and swimming. Can you bring something for blisters, bug bites and sunburn? ☐
>
> Love,
> Tyler

Topic Bank

1. Activities and injuries
2. Telling us what to do
3. Camp bunks
4. Camp food

Challenge: Pretend that you are somewhere far from home. Write a letter to someone back home. Write, in three paragraphs, what it is like where you are, what you miss back home, and what you really like about where you are. Don't forget to start with a salutation and end with a closing and signature.

For Younger Students: Create a form to direct students, and have them write a short letter to their parents or to an author whose books your class especially enjoys. You may take dictation from some students and allow them to illustrate their letters.

The Paragraph Work Sheet

You can use this paragraph worksheet any time you need to write a paragraph. It will work for any kind of paragraph. Follow steps 1–6. Write them on the lines below.

Paragraph Plan

1. Choose your main idea.

2. Choose your topic from the main ideas.

3. Narrow your topic.

4. Brainstorm. (Think of all the ideas you can about #3.)

5. Write a topic sentence.

6. Select the ideas you want to write about that go along with your topic sentence.

Example

1. pets

2. my hamster

3. My hamster makes me laugh.

4. He rolls around the floor inside a transparent ball, stuffs his cheeks full of grapes or nuts, washes himself strangely, spins around in his wheel, flips over out of his wheel, tickles with his whiskers, etc.

5. I named my hamster Bozo because he is like a clown, always making me laugh.

6. running in the wheel and the ball, stuffing his cheeks, and flipping over.

Your Paragraph Plan

1. Choose your main idea. _____

2. Choose your topic from the main ideas. _____

3. Narrow your topic. _____

4. Brainstorm. (Think of all the ideas you can about #3.) _____

_____

5. Write a topic sentence. _____

6. Select the ideas you want to write about that go along with your topic sentence.

_____

The Paragraph Checklist

❑ Did you brainstorm and come up with lots of ideas?

❑ Is your paragraph about only one idea or topic?

❑ Does your paragraph make sense?

❑ Are your sentences smooth and clear?

❑ Are all your sentences complete?

❑ Did you include good details, descriptions, and examples?

❑ Is your paragraph interesting? Will your readers be entertained or learn something?

❑ Have you checked for and corrected any spelling or grammatical mistakes you can find?

❑ Did you take out any sentences that do not belong?

❑ Have you rewritten your paragraph to make it better?

❑ Are your sentences arranged in an order (e.g., chronological order) that makes sense?

❑ Have you used transitions?

❑ Did you begin your sentences differently?

❑ Did you use lots of different kinds of sentences (some short, some long, etc.)?

❑ Is your writing fresh and original? Did you appeal to the senses in your descriptions?

❑ Did you use strong, active words?

❑ Is your paragraph neatly written so others can read it easily?

For Younger Students: Use only the first 3–7 for their checklists. Add more as they learn the concepts.

Paragraph Pass

Cut the Paragraph Pass strips from each page. Divide the class into groups of three. Distribute a strip to each group. On each strip, there is a topic sentence and three unfinished sentences. All group members read the topic sentence. Then each member of the group completes one helping, or body, sentence. All groups share their finished paragraphs with the class. This activity can be done many times, with the groups completing different strips or changing partners.

It's easy to make a peanut butter and jelly sandwich.	Some things make me laugh!
First, _____ _____ _____	What always makes me laugh is _____ _____
Then, _____ _____ _____	I start giggling when _____ _____ _____
Next, _____ _____ _____	I start laughing and can't stop when _____ _____ _____
Finally, _____ _____ _____	_____ _____ makes me laugh too!

Paragraph Pass *(cont.)*

There are lots of things to do on a rainy day.	Let me tell you about my favorite monster!
One thing is _____ _____ _____	I met my monster _____ _____ _____
You can also _____ _____ _____	My monster likes to eat _____ _____
Rainy days can be fun _____ _____	My monster looks like _____ _____ _____
Finally, _____ _____ _____	Lastly, my monster _____ _____ _____

Paragraph Pass *(cont.)*

Some things SCARE me!	It's easy to make a birthday cake.
I get scared when _____ _____ _____	First, _____ _____ _____
I also get frightened when _____ _____	Next, _____ _____ _____
What scares me the most is _____ _____	Last, _____ _____ _____
Finally, _____ _____ _____	And finally, _____ _____ _____

Paragraph Race

Students sit in four-member groups, in either rows or circles. There should be no talking during this activity.

Step 1. Person #1 writes a topic sentence and passes the paper to person #2.

Step 2. Person #2 writes a logical second sentence and passes the paper to person #3.

Step 3. Person #3 writes a logical third sentence and passes the paper to person #4.

Step 4. Person #4 writes a concluding sentence, proofreads the paragraph and brings the paragraph to the teacher.

Step 5. The teacher collects the paragraphs in the order received and reads them aloud. The first one turned in with all the correct steps wins first place, the second one gets second place, and so on. If playing with many attempts to write paragraphs (with teams rotating positions), assign points for each place and tally the total at the end of the race.

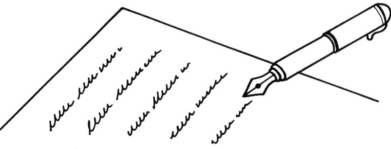

Challenge:

Mix and Write: Each student writes a topic sentence. The papers are mixed up and passed out so that each student writes the second sentence to a topic sentence he or she did not write, and so on until the papers have been mixed and passed four times. The completed paragraphs are read aloud in class.

Silly Write: Students write a topic sentence; then have each student fold the paper so that the topic sentence does not show. They should allow the last word or two of the topic sentence to appear below the fold so that the next writer has a bit of a clue. The next writer continues and allows a bit of his or her sentence to appear below the fold, and so on until the conclusion. When completed, the papers are unfolded and read aloud. See if any of them come close to making any sense!

For Younger Students: Have a team leader, a teacher, a parent, or an older student take dictation; or have each team prepare an oral paragraph presentation.

Scrambled Paragraphs

To prepare: Copy the sample paragraphs from below and the next page (or paragraphs you create on a computer's word processing program, using a large, easy-to-read font). Cut the sentences apart. (Paragraphs can be mounted and laminated before being cut, if you wish.) Be sure to make uncut copies of the paragraphs so that students can check them. For each group of four students, mix together the sentences of four different paragraphs. Let the students unscramble them and put the paragraphs back in order.

My favorite food is the marshmallow. It is white and fluffy like a pillow. It is gooey and sweet. It can be roasted over a fire, and then it is crunchy on the outside and sticky on the inside. I would like to eat a hundred of them for breakfast!

I have a very sleepy cat. She can fall asleep anywhere. One time she fell asleep inside my dad's boot. Yesterday she crawled into my sock drawer and slept there all day! We changed her name from "Frisky" to "Sleepy."

I don't like to swim. The water is cold and it gets up my nose. It also makes me tired. I hate it when I sink to the bottom. I am going to take karate lessons instead of swimming lessons.

Scrambled Paragraphs (cont.)

My sister is a slob. She leaves the caps off the pens. Her dirty clothes are on the floor. She eats pizza and leaves the crusts on the desk. I want my own room, okay?

I love to fly! Airports are very interesting places. It's really fun when the plane takes off. I can get to Grandma's house really fast in an airplane. I want to be an airline pilot when I grow up.

I don't like sodas. The bubbles make my throat and nose feel funny. When I finish drinking one of them, I burp. Sometimes when I open one, it sprays all over the place. I think I'll just drink water.

We have a very scary vacuum cleaner. It makes a scary, roaring noise. It chases me around the house. It has a light on it that looks like an eye. I refuse to vacuum my room!

I like to cook. First, I put on an apron that says, "Hug the Cook," and I then wash my hands. I like to create new dishes like peanut butter burritos. Last night I made chocolate spaghetti. No one in my family will try anything that I make.

The Paragraph-Matching Game

Cut out the topic sentence cards and the body sentence cards. Place them facedown. Each student alternates by turning over two cards. If they match, he or she takes the cards and tries again. If the cards do not match, they are turned back over and the next student gets a turn. A match occurs when a topic sentence makes sense when read with the body sentences on another card.

Topic Sentences

I have always wanted to ride an elephant.	I love to read.
My favorite season is summer.	Basements are scary.
My favorite food is pizza.	Grownups should go to school.
Toes are funny.	Grandparents are fun.

The Paragraph Matching Game *(cont.)*

Body Sentences

First of all, it would be really exciting. They are such big animals. Riding one would be exciting, being so high up there. It would be fun to tell all my friends that I rode an elephant.	They are always dark places. There are creepy-looking things in them like furnaces, water heaters, and old stuff. The creepy-looking things make scary sounds and have scary-looking lights on them. There are lots of cobwebs down there. I won't go down there.
First of all, there is no school in the summer, and I like that a lot! Second of all, there are lots of things to do like swimming, riding bikes, climbing trees, and baseball. Best of all, the sun stays up longer making things warm, and we can play until really late at night.	First of all, grownups don't know how hard school is or how much homework we have. They need to go to school so they will know how much work we have to do. They should try eating a soggy sandwich on the playground, too. Grownups need to go to school so they will understand what it's like for us.
It's my favorite food because I can find it anywhere or have it delivered. It's also my favorite food because it can have lots of different toppings on it, like tomatoes, olives, and even chocolate chips! But the most important reason why pizza is my favorite food is because it tastes really good!	They are nice and like to play with us. They let us eat whatever we want and never make us eat lima beans. They take us to the pizza place and the park. They give really big hugs and bake really good cookies. They have time for stories and pretending. I have fun at my grandma and grandpa's house.

Paragraph-Writing Tournament

Divide the class into teams of three or four. Give each team captain one of the topic sentence strips below. If you prefer, you may give each team captain the same topic sentence for each round. At your signal, the team captains go to the board to write the topic sentence. When the captain has finished, he or she hands the chalk to the next team member, who must write the first body sentence to support the topic sentence. The third team member writes the second body sentence or the concluding sentence (in the case of teams of three). With teams of four, the fourth team member writes the concluding sentence. As the paragraphs are completed, number them by writing #1 above the first, #2 for the second-place finisher, and so on. Once there is a paragraph on the board for each team, take a moment to read each paragraph aloud. The prizes (stickers, computer time, etc.) go to the team with the first paragraph completed with the least number of errors. Also, make sure that the paragraphs make sense and that the sentences do what they are supposed to be doing, either supporting the topic sentence or concluding the paragraph. If there is time, continue to play tournament style.

Broccoli is very strange.
Some dogs are very scary.
Summer is the best time of the year.
Everyone should have a teddy bear, even grownups.
Peanut butter is wonderful.
We should have school just one day a week.
Ears are good things to have.
Pets should wear clothes.
A very scary place is under a bed.
We should wear pajamas to school.

Paragraph-Writing Tournament *(cont.)*

A giraffe would make a good pet.
Lima beans are yucky.
A ball is the best toy ever invented.
Television is stupid.
We shouldn't have to clean our rooms.
It would be very difficult if we didn't have thumbs.
Grandpas are the best people in the world.
Airplanes are exciting!
Shoes are silly.
The best place to take a vacation is at the mountains.
We need lots of music.
The best way to eat ice cream is in a cone.
We need our eyebrows.
The world would be a different place if dinosaurs still lived.
The best foods are the sloppy ones.

Challenge: Make teams that have five or more members. Students may want to write their own topic sentences. Give them a timed period to write as many as they can think of. Collect them in a small box and allow team captains to draw a surprise topic sentence. (You may wish to screen them before actually beginning the activity.) Have two teams choose the same topic sentence, but have them choose opposing views on the topic. For instance, one team will write a paragraph about why ice cream is great, and another team will write a paragraph about why ice cream is not great. Introduce debate to your students.

For Younger Students: Divide the class into three-member teams. Give each team a topic sentence. (You may wish to use the same sentence for each team.) Allow the students to discuss their topic sentence and share their ideas. Provide clues if they need help. When they are ready, have the entire team come forward. One of the team members may write the sentences or you may take dictation from the team. Allow one team at a time to come forward. Then, when all the teams have had an opportunity to have a paragraph on the board, go over the paragraphs and award points for paragraphs that follow the guidelines.

Paragraph Maze

Find your way through the maze by making a paragraph. Some of the words in the paragraph are written right to left and bottom to top, so read carefully! Write the finished paragraph on a separate piece of paper.

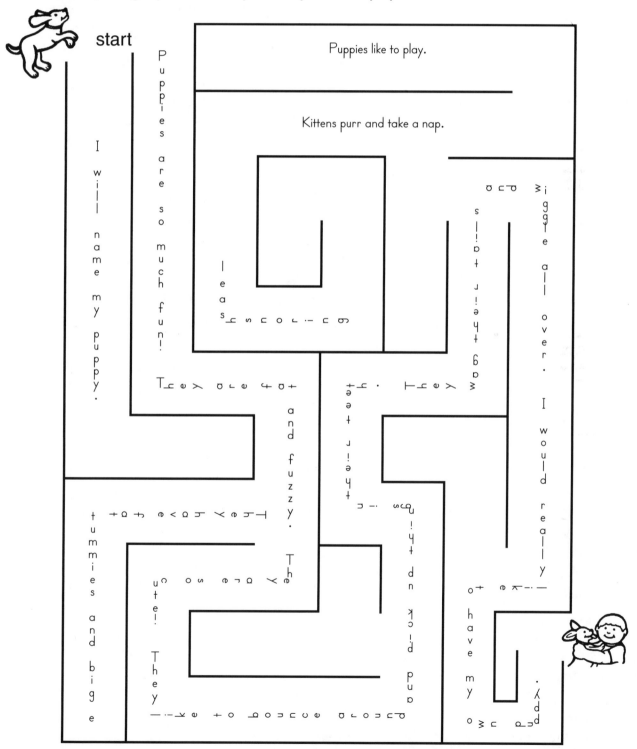

Answer Key

Page 8
1. television
2. favorite foods
3. toys
4. summer

Page 9
Things we find at home:
> table, rug
>
> sink, spoon

Weather:
> rain, fog
>
> snow, wind

Things we eat:
> spaghetti, ice cream
>
> cookies, apples

Things we wear:
> shirts, socks
>
> shoes, pajamas

Page 13
1. C
2. A
3. B

Page 17
Going to Camp
> 3 get on the bus
> 2 kiss parents good-bye
> 1 pack a bag

Eating Cereal
> 1 get a bowl
> 3 pour the milk
> 2 pour the cereal

Baking a Cake
> 3 put in the oven
> 2 pour the batter into a pan
> 1 mix the batter

Page 18
(Today,) I woke up early (and then) I brushed my (teeth.) (Next,) I put my homework in my backpack, (and then) I put my books in, too. I ate breakfast, (but then) I noticed that it was really quiet. (First,) I went to my mom's room, (but) she was still sleeping. (Next,) I went to my brother's room, (but) he was really asleep. (After that,) I went to the porch (and even) the dog was still sleeping. (Suddenly,) I remembered it was Saturday, (so) I went back to bed!

Page 22
The descriptive paragraphs:

There is a fuzzy, orange spider…

My seventh birthday is next week!…

Page 26
It looks like worms! (spaghetti)

It's really big and green, (a watermelon)

It's small and brown, (a teddy bear)

It's about the size of my foot (a sandal)

Page 34
Paragraph One: 2

Paragraph Two: 4

Paragraph Three: 1

Page 47
Puppies are so much fun! They are fat and fuzzy. They are so cute! They like to bounce around and pick up things in their teeth. They wag their tails and wiggle all over. I would really like to have my own puppy!